Poems by Nikki

Nichole Smith

Kingdom Builders Publications

Poems by Nikki

Copyright © 2014 Nichole Smith

Kingdom Builders Publications

All rights reserved. No part of this book may be reproduced or transmitted in any form or by any means without written permission from the author.

Library of Congress Control Number 2014915148
ISBN: 9780578149035

Photography
Franica J. Allison
Beat The Odds Photography LLC

Cover Designer
Franica J. Allison
Mark Linen
LoMar Designs

Editors:
Kingdom Builders Publications

Printed in USA

Go to our website: www.kingdombuilderspublications.com

Nichole Smith

This Book Belongs to

DEDICATION

This book of poetry is dedicated first, to my God Almighty. The words flowed from you whenever I prayed and asked your guidance with each piece. Your gift of words to me is such a tremendous blessing and I do not take it for granted. I look forward to making your name known in a greater way as your blessing name goes before me and prospers my way. It has always been my desire for people to contemplate you when they read my poetry. Thank you for your abundant goodness and leading me to a "Kingdom" minded publisher.

Secondly, this book is dedicated to my mother, Ivanette Williams Smith and my father, Calvin Smith. Mommy, although you are present with the Lord, your influence in my life lives on. Had it not been for the love you instilled in me for reading as a child, I could not be the writer that I am today. Thank you for always pouring life into me! You remain my greatest cheerleader and I am still humbled and awed by the depth of your love towards me. Daddy, thank you for being an awesome provider! It enabled us to buy the countless books we read as children. Even though I didn't always appreciate being asked to help you put your thoughts on paper as a teenager, it enabled me be the editor that I am today. Thanks, I love you, Hootie!

Thirdly, this book is dedicated to my uncle, Russell Linear Williams. You are the best uncle! You would give us $100 and tell us to go and buy whatever books we wanted. You always stressed the importance of education to us and helped foster a love for learning in us and gave liberally to anything educational that we wanted. Thank you! I love you.

Fourthly, this book is dedicated to my sisters: Natasha Raneé Smith and Terrie Terrale Wilson. You have always encouraged me to write and get published. Natasha, thank you for EVERYTHING! You are such a blessing to me. Terrie, thanks for staying on my case and giving me the big sister nudge, "Well hurry up and get published, then!" God's timing is perfect. I love you both!

Last but not least, this book is dedicated to Donna Morales, Waverney Herbert, Samantha Edwards, Karen Williams, Shari Buchanan, Patty Corder, Anna Stanfield, Dr. Keisha Gill-Jacob, Eunice Gill, Gina C. Edwards, Carla (Neise) Jefferson, Janelle Middleton, Reverends Elmer & Katrina Collins, and First Lady Glenda Bailey, Beat The Odds Photography, Kingdom Builders Publications, LLC., and Crystal Favor for your endless support and encouragement.

For I know the thoughts that I think toward you, saith the Lord, thoughts of peace, and not of evil, to give you an expected end. (Jeremiah 29:11, KJV)

BABIES
Inari
BIRTHDAYS
Co Pastor's Birthday
Dr. Owens
Sis Collins' Bday
DEATH
Bereavement
Loss
Samiya Cornelia Jones
Suicide
HOLIDAYS
Christmas
FAMILY
Amanda
Hootie
Amir
Amir 2
Dad's Poem
Sister Baby
FRIENDSHIP
A Divine Friendship
A Farewell to Lifelong Friends
A Friendship of Souls
A Kind Heart
A Good Spiritual Father
A Simple Gift
Alakeisha
Friends
I Care
Karen
Kitty
Moni
Shari
Simply Yvette
The Value of a Friendship
Reaching a Milestone (Tiff & Justin's Graduation)
Tinky
You, My Friend (You)
GODCHILDREN
Alicia (Soar)
Antoinette (Joy)
Timothy (Waiting for an email from Timothy)
GOODBYE'S
Frankie Myers
Goodbye, Tavis

HUMANITY
A Waste of Black Pride
Angel
First Love
God's Silver Lining
Mindful
Reminiscing
Secret Place
Square Seeds
Test
The Crossroad
When He Comes
MOTHERS
A Mother's Love
A Mother's Heart
A Present from the Heart
Mothers
PASTOR APPRECIATION
A Good Pastor
A Picture of Strength
A Ray of Sunshine
Elder
Fire and Ice
Honoring God's Servant
Just Being You
My Pastor
Servant Leaders
Servants
Sis Faye
Small Yet Mighty
Spiritual Father
Strength
Thanks
The Christ in You
The Light in Darkness
WEDDINGS
An Eternal Love
Bone of My Bone
Elaine
Jacob Vow Renewal
The Love I've Found In You
ANNIVERSARYS
Still Going Strong

CONTENTS

DEDICATION V

FOREWORD XI

A DIVINE FRIENDSHIP 12

A FAREWELL TO LIFELONG FRIENDS 13

A FRIENDSHIP OF SOULS 14

A GLORIOUS RESURRECTION 15

A GOOD PASTOR 16

A GOOD SPIRITUAL FATHER 17

A KIND HEART 18

A MOTHER'S LOVE 19

A MOTHER'S HEART 20

A PICTURE OF STRENGTH 22

A PRESENT FROM THE HEART 23

A RAY OF SUNSHINE 24

A SIMPLE GIFT 25

A TRUE FRIEND 26

A WASTE OF BLACK PRIDE 27

ALAKEISHA 28

SOAR 29

MY ENCOURAGER 30

AMIR: GRANDMOTHER TO GRANDSON 31

AMIR: MY SON, MY HEART 32

AN ETERNAL LOVE 33

ANGEL 34

JOY 35

BEREAVEMENT 36

BONE OF MY BONE	37
STILL GOING STRONG	39
JESUS IS THE REASON	40
A RENEWED FLAME	42
A MAN OF STANDARD	43
A GRATITUDE LOVE	44
GOD'S EAGLE	45
FIRE AND ICE	46
FIRST LOVE	48
GOOD-BYE FRANKY	49
FRIENDS	50
GOD'S SILVER LINING	51
GOODBYE TAVIS!	52
HONORING GOD'S SERVANTS	53
HOOTIE	55
I CARE	56
INARI	57
A PALPABLE LOVE	58
JUST BEING YOU	61
ENDURE	62
KITTY, A TRUE FRIEND	63
LOSS	64
LIGHT IN THE DARKNESS	65
MONI	66
MINDFUL	67
MOTHERS	68
MY PASTOR	70
REMINISCING	71
SUICIDE	72

SECRET PLACE	75
SERVANT LEADERS	76
SERVANTS	77
MY FRIEND	79
SIMPLY YVETTE	80
SIS COLLINS' BDAY	81
GRATITUDE FOR A VISION	83
MY SISTER BABY	85
SMALL YET MIGHTY	86
SPIRITUAL FATHER	88
SQUARE SEEDS	90
STRENGTH	91
TEST	93
THANKS	94
THE CHRIST IN YOU	95
THE CROSSROAD	96
THE DAY THE WIND CAME TO SCHOOL	98
THE ISSUES OF MY HEART	99
THE LOVE I'VE FOUND IN YOU	100
BECAUSE GOD IS OUR GUIDE	100
THE VALUE OF A FRIENDSHIP	101
REACHING A MILESTONE	102
TINKY	103
YOU, MY FRIEND	104
ABOUT THE AUTHOR	105

FOREWORD

Poetry is like the wind. It flows gently through the forest and touches each part of God's creation. The impact of its touch is soothing like a cool drink of water on a hot summer day. The writer of such work must have the first experience of its effect. Great writers such as Maya Angelou or Emily Dickinson had these encounters and flowed like the wind. I have read their works and been impressed with their vision and so it is with great resolve I adore the works of this author.

Nichole has been blessed with a tremendous gift to touch others with words. These works are like the wind. The vision of this writer is of a great visionary…one that has been touched and so touches others. The flow of the words reaches into the unknown parts of our being like the wind that touches the trees. The wind excites the trees to grow and produce, it excites the birds to fly, and it excites new life within a dense place. Words that are revealed by God are words of eternity that bring peace to the reader. The words of this book excite the mind and soothe the soul by gently touching the inner heart of all that read them. Anointed by God and revealed by his spirit, the hand that writes is the hand of God. He placed his hand over the hand of Nichole Smith and breathed revelation to touch others with a new desire. All that read will be blessed, all that read will be touched. Peace is like the gentle breeze within the forest of our mind, so is this book. Be blessed.

Rev. Elmer F. Collins

A DIVINE FRIENDSHIP

*Some connections are divine
Orchestrated from above,
In you I've found a friend
and we share a sisterly love.
You have been there for me
Throughout thick and thin,
Eternal is our bond
May it never end.
I appreciate who God made you
You're caring and filled with love,
You have a giving Spirit
That came from the Father above.
As you are honored today
Heaven and Earth rejoice,
When you start to speak
We hear the Lord's voice.
Continue to walk in your calling
Touching lives near and far,
Let God guide your footsteps
Enhancing all that you are.*

A FAREWELL TO LIFELONG FRIENDS

There are rare moments in life
When you meet a certain caliber of character
That leaves an impression on your soul
And you are forever changed by the occurrence...
Some people's gift from God
Is their ability to give love,
Demonstrating the nature of our Father
Which flows down from above.
The hearts that you have touched
As you've walked in this Way,
Are gathered as a gift to God
A beautifully fragrant bouquet.
Words cannot express
The gratitude that we feel,
For your servitude as you ministered
The Word in our hearts you sealed.
Your works unto the LORD
Reached beyond Dayton's walls,
To touch others in this Message
Unto which we've been called.
Describing you as blessings
Seems to belittle what you've done,
While fulfilling God's purpose
Oh, the many hearts you've won.
May the LORD go before you all
And ever prosper your way,
Farewell until we meet again
Here on earth, or on that Great Day!
God bless you my friends

A FRIENDSHIP OF SOULS

A great friendship is like the rays of the sun

Which warms everything in its path,

If you water and tend it as a garden

You can be sure that the harvest will last.

When trying to describe our friendship

I could barely type without tears,

Look at how the Father favored us

With each other's company throughout the years.

You have been the voice of Wisdom

Lifted my spirit when I was down,

Even mothered me at times

When mine could no longer be around.

There's a genuine sweetness about you

A joy bubbling from within,

As we celebrate your life today I can truly say

That I am blessed to call you my friend!

A GLORIOUS RESURRECTION

The agony of His death
The cruelty of the grave,
Every last drop of blood
Our suffering Savior gave.
How the Earth shook
And the sun lost its light,
The day Jesus became the ransom
For mankind's sinful plight.
But death could not hold Him
Within its unyielding grip,
Though He was brutally marred
By unbelief's cutting whip.
The Father heard
The Son's cry from hell,
Bowing the Heavens
As His Throne Chariot sailed.
Raising Him up from the depths below
Crowned both LORD and Christ
He sits at the right hand, you know?
His glorious resurrection
A testament to all,
That the power of God will lift us
No matter how far we fall.

A GOOD PASTOR

A good Pastor is hard to come by
Like a treasure you cannot find
A watchman over your soul
Until the end of time
Someone who feeds you the word
And all the truth that's there
If ever you carry a heavy load
It's something they are willing to share
Showing concern for your well being
When the road you travel gets rough
Letting you know that with prayer and faith
No trial is ever too tough
We appreciate your dedication
And the time you freely give
Thank you for showing us the way
God desires us to live.

A GOOD SPIRITUAL FATHER

A good father nurtures his child
And watches them grow
From a child to an adult
He counsels them and guides them
So also is a good Pastor
To his spiritual children…
How can we say thanks
For the many things you do
Lifting up our souls unto God
And helping us pray through
Pastor you are the epitome
Of an upright man
Giving us so much of yourself
And doing all that you can
Thank you for being obedient
And answering the LORD's call
We want to express our gratitude
For the Pastor and father you are to us all.

Nichole Smith

A KIND HEART

There are times when God blesses you

to demonstrate His love,

Surrounds you with lifelong friends

Angels straight from above.

Ours is a friendship

Of which I'm glad to be a part,

You are the epitome of goodness

And you've a kind heart.

Oh, the laughter we've shared

Joys and sorrows, too,

My life has been enriched

By the miracle that's you.

Your heart's desire be granted

By the Father that is our King,

And from time throughout eternity

May goodness to you He bring.

A MOTHER'S LOVE

A mother's love is a special gift

Straight from heaven above

She cares so much about you

And surrounds you with such love

She nurtures and takes care of you

Until it's time to set you free

And what's so special is even then

She won't really let you be

A mother's love forms a bond

That even time cannot sever

A mother's love is special

And yes, it's forever.

Nichole Smith

A MOTHER'S HEART

A mother's heart
Is a fragile thing,
Easily bruised
Often unseen.
Tirelessly giving
Pieces of itself away,
Overlooked countless times
Each day.
Steadfast, loyal
And loving to a fault,
Though many days
It's under assault.
From piercing words
And careless deeds,
When it begins to murmur
Please take heed.
Of how you mistreat it
And go on your way,
Without stopping to consider
The price you could pay.
For wounding
Such a vital tether,
It's the glue that holds
Your world together.
God must step in
And intervene,
Giving mom the transplant

She so desperately needs.
Providing life and
A blood transfusion,
As you watch
In desperate confusion.
Not realizing
That push had come to shove,
And you almost killed
What you really love.
Picture life
Without a mother's heart,
Oh, how your world
Would fall apart.
So open your eyes
Listen and look around,
Letting God guide you
To the joyous sound.
Of a mother's heart
Beating in love for you,
Denying itself
To help your dreams come true.
Treat it as
A tender rose,
Whose blossoms open
When kindness is shown.
Endeavor not
To take for granted,
The steadfast love
That God has planted.

Nichole Smith

A PICTURE OF STRENGTH

Strength of character in this day and age
Is oftentimes hard to find,
In a world consumed with serving itself
With its "I", "Me", "My", and "Mine".
But you arise as a beacon of Strength
In the midst a of restless crowd,
Holding up the bloodstained banner
As you cry aloud.
Ever pointing us to our Savior
As you fall on bended knee,
Interceding on our behalf
For the entire world to see.
Unashamed before God and man
To pour out your heart to the LORD,
Binding us together as the brotherhood
With love's unyielding cord.
Gratitude overflowing
From my heart it freely stems
And by God's grace & mercy
I'll follow you, as you follow Him.

A PRESENT FROM THE HEART

I wanted to get you a Christmas present
But nothing came to mind
For, I heard that giving is better than receiving
And I really enjoy being kind
You're a very special person
So, it is important to me
To get you something to surprise you
When you see it under the tree
But there is only one problem
That seems to stand in my way
I don't have any money
To get you a present on Christmas Day
So, what is it that I can give her?
My mind begins to ponder
That will bring a smile, happiness
And make the heart grow warmer
There is only one thing that I can give
And it comes straight from my heart
This poem that I am writing
I am sincere with every part
I hope that you enjoy it
And that it brightens up your day
I will end by saying
Merry Christmas, and may God always guide your way.

Nichole Smith

A RAY OF SUNSHINE

Thinking of you provokes a smile
That spreads from ear to ear,
And God is faithful to give me the words
To express my gratitude each year.
For the countless ways that you bless my soul
By giving yourself away,
Especially from the pulpit, ministering the Word
In your own unique way.
You have a style that's all your own
And believe me, none can compare,
You paint a picture with your words
And as you've taught us, favor ain't fair!
For it rests upon you from day to day
As you fulfill the Word of the Lord,
Teaching us never to leave home
Without sharpening our sword.
Lives you've touched and reasons you're loved
Are too numerous to count,
But appreciated to the fullest
Of that, have no doubt

A SIMPLE GIFT

A rose is really a simple gift

That seems to mean so much

Although it's something you can't keep long

And cannot often touch

It holds a wealth of meaning

Because it's given from the heart

For love and caring and sentiment

And friendships that just start

So consider yourself loved

If you receive a rose

It's the beginning of lifetime friendships

And from there…who knows?

Nichole Smith

A TRUE FRIEND

When I think of all of the blessings
and gifts from the Father above,
One that stands out the most
is the ability to give and receive love.
No one could have prepared me
for the true friend I've found in you,
How you have my best interest at heart
in all that you say and do.
You don't do things with fanfare
or to draw attention to yourself,
But your kind actions
are treasured more than wealth.
Your random acts of kindness
may seem miniscule to you,
But they are rays of God's love
always shining through.
Encouraging me in the midst of dark days
and making me lift my chin,
May your cup always overflow
with the love you give out, returning to you again.

A WASTE OF BLACK PRIDE

Lying dead in the streets
$200 dollar sneakers on your feet.
A waste of black pride.

My son, my son
Mama taught you to walk before you run.
A waste of black pride.

Nothing in this life is free
Though you may want it to be.
On the corner hustlin' that rock
Giving your own people culture shock.

Your whip has the rims
But, from whose blood do they stem?
A waste of black pride.

Seemingly having the best
Dozens of names tattooed across your chest.
A waste of black pride.

You swim in the blood of your own
High, broke, tired and alone
We thought the days of "massuh" gone,
Through dark clouds another face has shown
A waste of black pride.

ALAKEISHA

We've loved you, nurtured you,
And watched you grow.
You've blossomed into a beautiful,
Intelligent, compassionate woman of God.
We've watched you go through ups and downs,
Joys and sorrows.
Then, observed you rise up,
Stand on your fears, and conquer them…
Words seem too paltry to express
How proud we feel today,
Watching you enter into the next chapter of life
Spread your wings and start on your way.
Your journey is just beginning
To find what life is all about,
Put your trust in the Master
And His gifts He will bring out.
Our hopes and prayers you carry with you
Be a light wherever you go,
As you take the world by storm
We're going to sit back and watch the show!!
Alley, put God first and NOTHING can stop you! I love you.

SOAR

Step boldly into the destiny
That God has purposed for you,
Remember He has a plan
Weaved throughout all you go through.
Soar above situations
Reach up to the heights,
With Him as your focus
As you walk through life.
You project a tough exterior
But have such a fragile heart,
You've endured some things
That would cause others to fall apart.
As you sit on the Potter's wheel
A masterpiece in the making,
There is pleasure mingled with pain
As His nail scarred hands are shaping.
It is He who strengthens us
Through the trials we face,
And turns mourning into laughter
As the pain becomes erased.
I could not be there for every moment
But know you've always held my heart,
I am grateful for each chapter in your life
In which God let me be a part!

Nichole Smith

MY ENCOURAGER

When I reminisce of times spent with you
And lean upon the good,
You've always encouraged me
To be the best me that I could.
Life is less bright without you
No one could ever take your place,
Just thinking upon you
Brings a smile to my face.
When I wanted to give up you were there
To help me take one more step,
Words cannot express
The love within my heart's depth.
As I continue life's journey without you
I carry you within,
In every decision that I make
Your guidance knows no end.
Footprints left behind
Shoes too big to fill,
Permeating my every thought
Grandpa, you remain with me still.

AMIR:
GRANDMOTHER TO GRANDSON

My grandson, how can I tell you the depth of love that was born in me with your conception? How I prayed for you, warred for you, nurtured you from outside your mother's body until the Father breathed life and your spirit and soul took on a body and your eyes met mine for the first time. My heart leapt, my soul rejoiced, and our minds got joined to what our hearts already knew...this is love. Unconditional, full to brimming, my cup ran over with the wonder of you. So small and yet so strong. So weak, and yet so purposed, that warring angels took up your cause and battled back that which the enemy thought to destroy you, me, oh yes, all of us with. Ha! Nevertheless, God's hand never left cradling you in the palm of His mighty, yet tender hand upholding you through all that death tried to ensnare you with. And here you stand, growing, living, learning, giving and demonstrating the very thing which was almost, (pause with hands extended in praise), yes, almost was taken from you....LIFE.

I choose to live and NOT die!

AMIR:
MY SON, MY HEART

My son, so much a part of me, your hurts are my hurts, your pains, my pains. When you smile, my heart grows wings and soars. How could I have prepared myself for the love that would spring forth out of so much pain? People, with their opinions tried to form and speak on my destiny, your destiny, our destiny; from the beginning. Lack of understanding of the Father's divine plan for me...for you, yes, for us. How the light of God pierced my soul and shined for you, yet within my womb. Causing the warrior in you to rise up and defy the ineffective words of naysayers. A warrior you were destined to be as you are descended from warrior blood. A Warrior-Bride is your destiny, your majesty, the royalty we're called to be. Entwined natures of Lion and Lamb, descendants of the Great, "I AM." On a pilgrimage to the Promised Land, aptly named, New Jerusalem. No one can stop what God ordained though the enemy reaches time and again. Grasping nothing but air as God lifts you high. Though separate, we're one, you and I. My love for you, you cannot yet fathom... God kept my mind when it could have been lost, thinking I might lose you, counting the cost. But God preserved you just for me and flaunts your story for His majesty. He who was, and is, and is to come, marvel at a work not yet done. For it remains to be seen who you are in Him, a jewel, a royal diadem. My love for you will never waver, He's holding us, our mighty Savior. I'll just keep praying, watch and see, as He makes you what He purposed you to be...

AN ETERNAL LOVE

Love is eternal
Some even say divine,
It remains unending
Despite passage of time.
Ebbing and flowing
As waves of the sea,
Divine appointment
Led you to me.
From the hands of our Creator
Whose nature is love,
Our paths crossed
Guided from above.
Before form
Our bodies took,
I belonged to you
From our first look.
'Ere the moment we met
My heart leapt inside,
A seed started growing
And never broke stride.
No matter distance or circumstance
It patiently grew,
As I traveled, life's journey
Led me to you.
United as one
A new life we start,
Tread carefully, love
For you carry my heart.

ANGEL

An angel touched me on my brow

Early one Sunday morning

Just a whisper of a touch awakening me

As the day was dawning

I squinted to get a glimpse of it

But this was not meant to be

A fraction of a glimpse as it disappeared

Is all I was allowed to see

But this was enough to give me a taste

Of what lies down the road

When all my trials and tribulations are over

And my burdens I'll unload

The path of righteousness is difficult

So were the sins Jesus had to bear

But wherever I go from now on

I'll have an angel with me there.

JOY

The thought of you warms my heart
And brings a smile to my face,
Though distance may separate us
Memories can never be erased.
The joy I feel when I see you
Is renewed each time,
Like finding hidden treasure
The experience is sublime.
From the moment of your birth,
You have always been a "cutie",
As the years have passed
It's undeniable you're a beauty!
The thing I love the most is
It's not just on the outside,
But radiates from deep within
Impossible to hide.
Even when I can't visit
I carry you with me every day,
My prayer is that you'll be led by the Master
Each step along the Way.
There's a grace that is upon you
A compassion in all you do,
I can't wait to see the end result
Of what God molds you into.

BEREAVEMENT

Life is a fragile thing

Whose length is in God's hands

And we must remember

That death is part of His Master Plan

Losing a loved one

Is a hard thing to bear

And in your time of need

We just want you to know we care

So if you need a shoulder to lean on

Or a helping hand

Remember that we love you

And will help any way we can.

BONE OF MY BONE

This is now bone of my bone
and flesh of my flesh
ordained by the Creator above,
God took a rib and as Adam slept
closed the flesh instead thereof.

Two hearts made one
two halves whole
two lives now made complete,
Praise God that in eternity past
it was purposed that we meet.

A love deep and infinitely rich
as boundless as the skies,
Individuality disappears
when gazing into your eyes.
Fears conquered; a journey starts
with love to pave the way,
How our hearts are intertwined
as we take our vows today.

The Heavenly hosts rejoice with us
at the fulfillment of God's plan,
The LORD himself is smiling down
as we are joined by His hands.

Unique is our union and blessed are we
to have found each the love of our life,
God's grace envelopes us
as we become husband and wife.

Words cannot fully express
the depth of what we feel,
Since entering each other's lives
our hearts have now been healed.

Each day spent together in the years ahead
is a gift from God above,
May our marriage ever be
a reflection of His precious love.

STILL GOING STRONG

Ten years ago we said "I do"
And began a uniting of souls,
One thing I've learned about you
Is that you have a heart of gold.
Baby, you bring my life
Balance, comfort, and joy
My love for you is deep
About that, I couldn't be coy.
Although you are strong
There's a tenderness you revealed to me,
You opened up your heart
Laying it bare so that I could see.
The love you express through giving
The commitment you display to our Lord,
The way you protect our family
Like a warrior wielding a sword,
What started ten years ago
Is a flame still going strong,
With you by my side in this life,
I know we can't go wrong.

JESUS IS THE REASON

What a fantastic time

To celebrate His birth,

Oh, what a sweet Savior

Come down to earth.

Leaving a throne

What a majestic King,

To love us so much that

Salvation He'd bring.

By humbling Himself

To walk among sinful man,

For three-and-a-half years

He taught all He can.

But sadly some

Still never believed,

His message of love

They did not receive.

Until God let Him hang high

On a blood soaked Cross,

Then to the very depths of hell

To redeem the lost.

With victory He rose

All power in His hand,

Now He sits with the Father

And rules the lands.

Of willing hearts and minds

That acknowledge Jesus is the reason

It is He who gave the privilege to celebrate

CHRIST*mas* this season!

MERRY CHRISTMAS!!!

NEVER FORGET THAT HIS BLOOD BOUGHT ALL CREATION!!

A RENEWED FLAME

The wonder of you is amazing
You took me by surprise,
I just wasn't prepared
For the love shining from your eyes.
There are many things about you
That distinguish you from the rest,
You make me feel safe and warm
Your big heart is what I love best.
You comfort me and make me happy
A peacefulness is within,
Today I stand and marry
Someone who is my friend.
I love everything about you
You're kindhearted and sweet,
God directed our lives
It was purposed that we meet.
You are caring and loving
The way you look at me warms my heart,
From this moment on
It's till death do us part.
You're it for me
I'll never be the same
In the light of your love I've discovered
An ever burning, renewed flame.

A MAN OF STANDARD

You are an inspiration
To everyone you meet,
Even though you're direct
Most times you're down right sweet.
You protect your loved ones
With the fierceness of a king,
And guide your spiritual children
Through the Word you bring.
Ever since I met you
You've challenged me,
To reach forward to that
Which I was called to be.
As we celebrate your birth
The angels in Heaven rejoice,
For the lives which you help transform
Simply by using your voice.
Sightless you see further
Than the outward appearance of man,
Looking within to the spirit
Sculpting it to fit God's Plan.
Enjoy your day to the fullest
Basking in the honor you're due,
Today is set aside
To celebrate you!

A GRATITUDE LOVE

Some things enhance with age
For us, that's certainly true,
I'm as excited as the day we met
To renew my vows with you.
A union ordained by God
We were set up from above,
As we've stepped from days to years
The deeper and richer our love.
Our paths, once separate
Now entwined by circumstance,
I'm so glad our marriage
Wasn't an occasion of happenstance.
What love the Father felt
To enrich my life with you,
There to lift my head
Our Creator to point me to.
Grateful for this love
He's entrusted us to share,
No matter what life brings
I know you're always there.
I have a gratitude for you, my love
That words can't adequately express,
I lift eyes heavenward and smile
Knowing I've been blessed.

GOD'S EAGLE

You are God's appointed eagle
Not just soaring through the heavens above,
But serving here upon earth
Ministering His Word in love.
A guardian of God's sheep
Spiritual Father to many,
Pouring life out unto all
Not willing to lose any.
The caliber of your teaching and preaching
Is in a class all by itself,
The storehouse that you pull from
Holds untold spiritual wealth.
The numerous lives you have touched
The tireless ways that you give,
You unselfishly share your strength
So that others may live.
These words are small in comparison
To the great work of God that you do
Words cannot express
How highly we think of you.
We hope that your birthday is great
Filled with lots of fun,
You may be District Two's elder
But to us…you're number one!

FIRE AND ICE

God's nature is both fire and ice, exaltation and humility . It is seen throughout creation. Our Pastors embody these attributes.

She is *"eesh"*, the fiery side of man,

Her passion for the LORD is vibrant

Enabling her to push him to heights no one else can.

He is humility, the quiet force within her storm,

When the billows are raging

He protects her from all harm.

Entrusted with God's flock

A garden comprised of souls,

Watchmen in perilous times

No matter how the warfare unfolds.

Grooming a Spiritual bride

Aw-bad servants unto the LORD,

Pressing onward and upward

Eternal gain is the reward.
Fire is able to change
The nature of a thing,
Ice is able to soothe
No matter how fierce life's sting.

We can never thank you enough
For feeding us the Word,
Even when it seemed
As if you weren't heard.
God bless you richly
From time through eternity,
Until we look into the face of love
Becoming that which we have seen.

eesh – Hebrew for the firey side of man

Nichole Smith

FIRST LOVE

I didn't know I was capable of loving anyone

Until I met you,

And by the time I figured it out

I really didn't know what to do.

I tried to tell you in simple ways

A caress, a smile, an embrace,

I'm sure that if you looked close enough

You'd see it written all over my face.

Whenever I catch sight of you

My heart beats really fast,

I don't think I can hold back any longer

I don't know how long I can last.

Someone said, "I love you more than words can say"

Well, in my case it's true,

But there are three words I have to say

And those are I love you.

GOOD-BYE FRANKY

Franky, you're one of a kind

We all agree that's true,

And we just wanted to say

How much 5th grade will miss you.

You're a guy with style

And have your own special flare,

We couldn't send you to New Jersey

Without saying how much we care.

You will be truly missed

Knowing you has been great,

These pictures will remind you of Maryland

And all of the memories you have yet to create.

FRIENDS

When I think about you, I have to smile

You're one of the nicest people I know

Always a hug and a smile to give

No matter where you go

You always have an encouraging word to give

Something sweet to say

And every time I see you

It brightens up my day

I'm glad I had the chance to meet you

An opportunity to be your friend

And I hope the friendship we have

Will never, ever end.

GOD'S SILVER LINING

God's silver lining isn't something
That we can always see
Because His reasons and His thoughts
Are higher than we
Our trials and tribulations
Are but a means to an end
The pathway to heaven
Does not twist or bend
Through the muck and the mire
And the burdens we bear
God's silver lining
Is always there
A light into our path
and a lamp unto our feet
God's silver lining is with us
Through every trial we meet
So, when life throws you a curve
And something gets you down
Remember God's silver lining
Is always around.

Nichole Smith

GOODBYE TAVIS!

You are such a little gentleman
You have a style all your own,
The year has been so fun
And boy, how you've grown.
From Mrs. Kidd's class to Ms. Armour's
Changes have been plenty,
From Mr. Chapman to Miss Smith
The lives you've touched are many.
We will miss your singing
And all the hugs that you give,
Monkey-style at recess
Now that's the way to live!
Utah might make you laugh
The way that Marylanders do,
Remember the fun we had
And how much we love you!!

HONORING GOD'S SERVANTS

An awesome dedication

Unfailing commitment

Unending loyalty

And a willingness to serve

Pastors, shepherds, servants,

And friends…

We want to honor the man and woman of God today,

Though words are poor substitutes

For all that we can say.

Your years of service,

Surrenders, and love,

For sharing your gifts

Given from above.

For times of pain,

Struggles, and sorrow,

Going on

Despite what may come tomorrow.

How can mere thanks

Encompass all that you do?

Standing in the gap
And carrying us through.
The highs, the lows,
The good, the bad,
Times of binding together
This family has had.
Taking time to give honor
Where honor is due,
A bouquet of love
We hand to you.
A token of thanks,
Smiles, and deeds,
In gratitude for
The awesome call that you heed.

HOOTIE

There are so many words to describe you dad
That I just couldn't pick one,
And even though your birthday was yesterday
I decided to give you a weekend of fun.
You are an excellent provider
We've had some great family time,
When God was handing out dads
I'm glad that you chose to be mine.
We have seen a lot of the world
Because you wore army boots,
When it comes to making us laugh
You really are a hoot!
Through times good and bad
We ultimately stick together,
Love supersedes all
It remains the strongest tether.
Hootie, we just love you
From young to old,
We are grateful for your sacrifices
You have a heart of gold.

Nichole Smith

I CARE

The precious way you touch my heart
Is something I can't explain
I only know I long for this feeling
Again and again
My love is as delicate as a flower
As gentle as a rose
And every time I look at you
The stronger and deeper it grows
You mean so much more to me
Than the words I write express
Each look you send me shows you care
And fills me with tenderness
I wish I could put you inside of me
And show you how I feel
Letting you see that secret part of my heart
That was yours all along to steal
I know you'll never fully understand
The way I feel about you
But, then, perhaps I'm wrong and you can
For if you love me, surely, you feel it, too.

INARI

Babies are a gift from God
A precious, eternal gift,
They can always make you smile
And give your heart a lift.
Innocent is their nature
And carefree is their heart,
We are gathered here today
To celebrate Inari's start.
We raise you up unto the LORD
And give you back to Him,
Creator of the Universe
From whose blood you stem.
May God bring to fruition
All He's purposed you to be,
Seeds planted by God
Fruits that all will see.
You are so dear to us
Our hearts could literally burst,
You're second to none in our family
Inari, you're first.

JACOB VOW RENEWAL
A PALPABLE LOVE

Wife, companion, confidant, and my best friend:

When I look back on our lives, it is hard to imagine what it would have been like without you. You are always pushing me to greater heights. You are not just concerned with your dreams, you encourage me to dream with you. I am grateful.

When it comes to virtuous women

Love, you exceed them all,

You're there to lift my head

To support me when I fall.

The depth of what you mean to me

No words can ever express,

Anyone touched by the rays of our love

Doesn't have to ask if I'm blessed.

Your love for me is apparent

In everything that you do,

I continuously talk to our Father

Thanking Him for gifting me, you.

You embraced my children

And mothered them as your own,

Taught them the wisdom of uniting as family

And if they have each other they're never alone.

You are my rib

The missing part of me,

I marry you again today

For all the world to see.

Husband, my rock, my backbone, and my best friend:

How time has flown! It seems as if only yesterday you were returning to the neighborhood and I was knocking on your door…you answered…and my life has never been the same. I am grateful. No one knows our story better than us.

We've been through the fire together

Weathered many a storm,

You've comforted me in the bad times

And sheltered me from harm.

With you, I've never been stifled

You gave me wings to fly,

I fall deeper in love with you
As the years go by.
Each milestone with you is a testament
Of God's great love for me,
Your heart is as big as an ocean
Your compassion as deep as the sea.
You fathered my daughters
Protected them as your own,
They've blossomed thanks to your strength
Look at them now, they're almost grown.
Vessels in the hands of the Potter
He joined us both together,
I commit myself to you again this day
We will walk hand in hand forever.

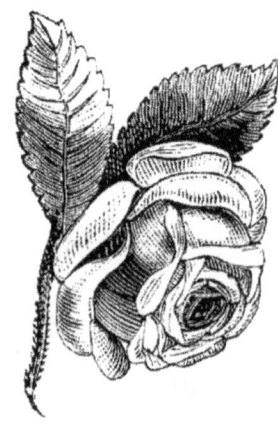

JUST BEING YOU

How can we say thank you
For all that you've done
The laughter and tears
The sadness and fun
Your anointing is special
A rare gift indeed
To be appointed keeper
Of God's bride seed
Thank you for moments
Given each day
And for all of those times
You went out of your way
To help us pray through
A hardship or trial
And for comforting us
When your number we dialed
Thanks for your obedience
To the great "I am"
Whether He's using you as a lion
Or a meek little lamb
We appreciate all
Of the things you do
But thanks most of all
For just being you.

Nichole Smith

ENDURE

Our friendship will endure
From time to eternity,
Words cannot express
All that you mean to me.
You have picked me up when I'm down
Made me smile through my tears,
Caused me to see the brighter side
Put it in reverse and switch gears.
You never fail to make me laugh
And place a smile on my face,
We've shed many a tear
Speaking of the LORD's grace.
You've a wisdom beyond your years
And you're sassy to boot,
If I chose a phrase to describe you
I'd have to say you're a hoot!
I am grateful to our Creator
That knit our spirits together,
With His love from above
It is a never fraying tether.

KITTY, A TRUE FRIEND

People pass through life
Never touching the lives of another,
But sometimes God gives a friend
That sticks closer than a brother.
You are a light in darkness
A joy to all you meet,
Whether it be family
Or someone you pass on the street.
Your laughter reaches down deep
And lightens the burdened heart,
You're tops in my family's book
Of the Smith clan you'll always be a part.
When we faced the death of my mother
You were a friend on which we could lean,
There for all of us
Working behind the scenes.
We are honored to celebrate
Your birthday today,
You are always in our prayers
As you walk in the Way.
There are some things in life
That just don't come to an end,
Such is the love
Of a loyal, true friend!

Nichole Smith

LOSS

In your time of grief

Our thoughts are with you

Throughout all that you say

And all that you do

There are no words to express

The sorrow we feel

But memories of Clytie

Are with us still

Try to be happy

And keep a smile on your face

Because we all know

She's in a better place.

LIGHT IN THE DARKNESS

You are a light in the darkness

A fresh spring breeze

Your holiness is visible

As the LORD you seek to please

You bring a smile to my face

When I see you running on

You're an example, and you remind me

The battle is already won

Thank you for your time

And the words of wisdom that you share

It's nice to know

That you really care.

Nichole Smith

M O N I

There's something special I see in you

Something shared between us two

It can only be found deep inside two friends

Take time to care and to mend

The friendship that daily grows

As beautiful as the rose

Of course there are thorns along the way

That may cause priorities to stray

But that's what makes a friendship strong

And in that there can be no wrong

There's nothing I know that is more true

Than the faithful friend I've found in you

And with God's care and watch from above

Between us there will ever be a friend's love.

MINDFUL

Make the best of your time

Be a blessing to someone's day

Help to lift someone up

With something you do or say

Think about the day that's left

Instead of the day that's past

Get your house in order

Before the die is cast

Give a kind word or deed

It's simple enough to do

And remember to, "do unto others

As you would have them do unto you."

Nichole Smith

MOTHERS

Who knows the heart of a Mother

Better than the Father above,

For He it was that created

That endless wellspring of love.

There is none throughout all creation

Who is treasured such as she,

No one that can take life from a thought

And birth it to be.

She is God's earthly womb

Filled with tender care,

It matters not if you belong to her

She has love enough to share.

A Mother is an extension

Of God's heart which beats for the world,

Please don't take it for granted

It is a priceless pearl.

In times of good and bad

Seasons of pleasure and pain,

Your Mother is a constant

Her support an endless refrain.
Pushing you to your greatest heights
As she watches with bated breath,
Just in case you stumble
When it's time to leave her nest.
Love her while she's with you
Honor her if she has passed,
For the gift that God bestowed unto you
The memories of a great Mother always last.
So to Mothers near and far
Your worth is beyond compare
Know that you are loved
You are treasured, you are rare.

Nichole Smith

MY PASTOR

How do I describe you when
So many words come to mind
A woman of patience and longsuffering
Who's most assuredly kind
A mother for those who need one
But certainly a teacher, too
Sit still and listen my child
As she breaks the Word down to you
With a joy that's visible inside and out
Come on Holy Ghost, have your way
People, you have to get out of the flesh
And let the LORD use you today
My pastor is available night and day
She's guided by the Spirit of the LORD
And if you're doubtful she'll let you know
With God's help nothing is too hard
I thank God I have a Pastor like her
To lead and guide my way
And I just want to let her know
Pastor, I love you today.

REMINISCING

Thinking of you never fails

To bring a smile to my face

And makes me wish you were near

For me to embrace

My head may forget

But my heart never will

The feelings we shared

Are with me still

Lingering in my soul

Brightening my day

No one but you

Made me feel this way

Even though we've parted

You are with me still

And a part of my heart

You will always fill.

SUICIDE

In times of mourning, so bittersweet
You long to touch and to hold
The person whom you've just recently lost
And will never see to grow old
At first it hurts and tears you apart
You feel like you want to die, too
Then, you get mad and start to blame God
Wondering why He's taken them from you
But death is ten times worse the hurt
Way down deep inside
When it turns out the person that's gone
Has committed suicide
Death is no joke, that you can be sure of
And it happens from day to day
What has gone so wrong on this earth?
That someone would choose to take their life that way
It is something I think I will never understand
But I hope comes to an end
For I will never forget the way her life was taken
The life of a very dear friend.

OUR ANGEL

The sweetness of your smile

The sound of your laugh,

Our angel come to Earth

As you walked life's path.

Watching you grow

Counting your fingers and toes,

Seeing things through your eyes

Wondering what each day will hold.

Such a blessing you are

What a joy unto our hearts,

We love you always

Though circumstances caused us to part.

God called your name

And angels carried you on High,

It seems too soon

To have to tell you goodbye.

Heaven is brighter

Because it has you there,

Our Lord received you

And holds you within His care.

In our hearts you'll live on

From our memories never part,

This wasn't the end of life for you

Praise God…it was just the start!

SECRET PLACE

Sometimes I need a secret place
To hide and go away
To visit for a moment
Or perhaps to spend the day
A place that only I can reach
Somewhere to call my own
It's almost like stepping right outside
Just further away from home
Who knows what I may see or do?
That's what makes it fun
I might need to talk to the LORD
Personally, one on one
And hold his hand and think about
What he's done for me
To have Him lift a burden I carry
And just didn't see
To bring a smile and happiness
There may be tears, too
In order to relieve the stress
Of what I'm going through
So, I'll continue to visit my secret place
Until the day I die
Or until the LORD comes back
And cracks open the sky.

SERVANT LEADERS

As we gather to celebrate
The Resurrection of our glorious King,
I am thanking God
For the precious Word that you bring.
Shepherds over a flock
Entrusted to you from eternity past,
Only the Word will remain
Nothing else will last.
Thank you for being His servants
Guiding us through these perilous times,
Truly in these last days
Christ is our paradigm.
As we worship the Lamb
Who was slain for our sin,
May the cords of His love bind us
The eternal Brotherhood never end.
Thank you for your sacrifice
To our risen LORD,
May our sho-far trumpets resound
In melodious accord.

SERVANTS

Leading us to still waters

With a firm but gentle hand,

Guiding us into worship

As we follow the Slain Lamb.

Carrying the weight of the mantle

Leading us unto the cleft,

Surrounding and protecting

Ensuring no sheep is left.

As we journey onward and upward

The Master we pursue

We are grateful

God chose our shepherds to be you.

He has added another year

To each of your lives,

Only God knows

The depth of your sacrifice.

Birthdays are special times

Life celebrations,

God must smile

When looking down on His creations.

Thanks for all that you do

For the plethora of ways that you give,

True servants of God

Reflected in the way that you live!

We Love You!!

MY FRIEND

Whenever I think of our friendship
It never fails to bring a smile,
Seems as if we've known each other forever
Instead of a little while.
Your kindness touches my heart
And makes me strive to do more,
Friends should stretch you to your next level
That's one of the things they're for.
You are such an encouragement
Can always turn my frown upside down,
Besides all of that
You're just plain fun to be around.
My heart bubbles over
From all the joy that you send,
It is truly a pleasure to call you my friend.
I'll give you your flowers now
Envision a beautiful bouquet,
I just felt like it was my turn
To put a smile on your face today!

SIMPLY YVETTE

You have a smile
That radiates like the sun,
We've shared lots of laughter
Had a lot of fun.
I appreciate your friendship
And love you just for being you,
Your personality...
You're loyal as well as true.
Some people just enhance your life
Make brighter your days,
Ever since I met you
You've blessed me in so many ways.
No matter distance or time
You are there,
Blessing me with your wisdom
Showing me you care.
I rejoice with the Heavens
As we celebrate your birth,
There aren't enough words
To adequately express your worth!

SIS COLLINS' BDAY

We have come together

To help celebrate your day,

And express our gratitude

For all that you do and say.

A birthday tends to make

One look at times past,

A lifetime of memories

Moments that will last.

We celebrate the unique person

That God made you,

Changing our lives with the Word

And spreading joy with the things that you do.

Who else has you laughter?

Your style, your flair,

We really appreciate

The ways you show that you care.

God chose us to be family

Some of us are even kin,

All of these years together

Has caused us to be friends.

So we hope you've had a ball

And enjoyed yourself to the core,

Happy Birthday, Sis Collins

And many, many more!!

GRATITUDE FOR A VISION

How can you thank someone

For grasping hold of a vision?

A divine inspiration, heavenly revelation.

That was waited for and tarried over

As the Holy Ghost tarries over us.

An ear bent like a bowl, intently tuned

Waiting for the still, small voice

Of Almighty God to breathe into it.

Natural eyes closed, spiritual open

A heart that is soft and pliable

Seeking, searching, waiting.

Hands open and uplifted, waiting to be filled

With works sent from Eternity past.

Knees bent, shoulders ready

To receive the burden placed upon them.

Feet ready to walk circumspectly before Him

Ever following a bloodstained path.

A mouth filled with honey, butter, and oil

A will bowed in humble submission,

A soul filled with tranquil trust.

Bless you for all that you do

To bring this joy to pass,

Memories of Heaven touched here

Long after we've returned home, will last.

May the LORD always overflow your cup

And cause you to move in His will,

These paltry words seem inadequate

For the gratitude that we feel.

As you leave this place today

Know that you are dearly loved,

Not just here on earth

But by Our Father who dwells above.

MY SISTER BABY

What can I say about you?
You're crazy, you're funny, and you're kind,
Girl, you've got a brain
That I sure wish was mine!
You are an awesome teacher
Your students are very blessed,
I admit you've got skills
I mean…Muck let you shave his chest ☺
I'm grateful to call you my sister
You've been there through thick and thin,
The thing that makes me smile the most
Is that you're my best friend.
We argue, we fight, we disagree
Get tight-lipped and walk away,
But when it's all said and done
We make up by the end of the day.
I feel like God gave me a twin
Even though we're two years apart,
I've told you this before
You're the sister of my heart.

Nichole Smith

SMALL YET MIGHTY

The LORD's Master Plan is unknown

And often times we cannot see,

The things that the Father purposed

To flow from time to eternity.

This ministry was birthed

As a small humility seed,

Entrusted to your Pastor's heart

For God knew he would believe.

Enough to water it with tears

When the fruits were yet unknown,

To protect it from wayside soil

As from promise to performance it grows.

Faith filled a basement

And spilled into the streets and abroad,

People came from all over

Tell me, who could do that…but God?!

Don't even be fooled by this building

That you see before you today,

It's just a pit stop on your journey

As Word Alive Worship Center makes its way;

To The destiny that God cradled

In his hands with tender care,

Knowing that with your combined faith

He'd be able to bring you there.

Mighty in the Kingdom

Though small was your start,

You are treasured by the Father

A delight unto His heart.

He knew that He could trust you

Not to withhold His Word from any,

Faithful over a few things

Purposed to be ruler over many!

SPIRITUAL FATHER

What caliber of man is a Spiritual Father?

What qualities does he possess

which qualify him to wear the dual hats

of spiritual and natural father?

Loyalty is sure to reside in his heart

while courage surrounds it.

Longsuffering assuredly pumps through his veins

and flows from his being to touch others.

His hands are full with the burdens of others

he lifts up to the Father.

His arms are strengthened from holding not only

himself up, but others.

His head is beautiful and full of wisdom

because he has sought the mind of the Master.

His eyes glow with the light

of the LORD's love.

His ears are like bowls,

which are full of the instruction of God.

His lips are full of skillful words

as they part with butter, honey, and oil.

His knees have been strengthened

from fervent prayer.

His feet are shod with the preparation

of the Gospel of peace.

Pastor, you possess all of these qualities and more.

God bless you

on this Father's Day and always.

SQUARE SEEDS

In days gone by and times past, we made a choice and the die was cast. Catapulted through space we strive here in time, praying our choices have reason or rhyme. Square seeds reaching, never fitting in, searching, and searching past inherent sin. For the light, which calls forth the flower's bloom as it narrowly escapes, intended doom. Onward and upward, staying its course, the Kingdom suffereth violence, but the violent TAKE it by force.

STRENGTH

When thinking of words to describe you

Strength just seemed to fit

Your dedication to the people of God

The way you never quit

You have a quiet way

That calms the raging storm

When it comes to Pastors

Your caliber is above the norm

At my crucial moments in life

You remind me to look to God

And never to start the day

Without having my feet shod

Your faithfulness to the Lord's cause

Is inspirational to me

Opening blinded eyes

Causing the world to stop and see

The vision of our Lord

Breadths, lengths, heights, and depths

The brilliant light of the Word

Truly, our souls have been kept

You're God's man

Endlessly pursuing His heart

Your ministry is such

That I'm blessed to take part

In the fabric being weaved

The tapestry of our King

As you teach us to lift Him high

His praises ever sing

Happy birthday, Pastor

I pray you have many more

For I can't wait to see

What else God has in store!

TEST

Lord, people keep pressing me
and I know it's you testing me
to see if I will yield to what I feel
or wrestle within my vessel
to make your glorious Name known.
You know the love in my heart,
from your Word I will not part
for it guides me daily to your light.
So I won't disgrace you by asserting
what I think to be my rights...because truly, I have none.
All that I have and am
and shall be is due to you.
I will ever give your Name the glory
for one round with my flesh is not the end of the story!
Victory was wrought at Calvary by the power of your blood
working ever for my good
let's make sure it's understood
...no matter the test...I AM YOURS!

THANKS

When the road gets long and the weight is heavy

From the burdens you have to bear

Remember you have pillars within the church

Saints who really care

People God has raised up

Who are willing to fill their slots

People who desire to be real

And don't pretend they're something they're not

We are blessed to have you as our leader

A Pastor after God's own heart

And whenever you need help

We will willingly do our part

So lean on us when times are rough

Using the strength that keeps us living

We'll support you as you follow Christ

Because its life through the word you've given.

THE CHRIST IN YOU

Your light has touched my soul

And brought forth a light in me

Watching you walk the Crucified Way

Shows me how I should be

Your faith is inspirational

And strengthens my inner man

It is powerful to know

That I'm in God's holy plan

Whenever I get discouraged

You reach out and touch my hand

And say, "Sister Nikki, I love you today

If I made it I know you can"

I hope that in some way

I'm an inspiration to you

And as I grow closer to God

You can see my light shining, too.

Nichole Smith

THE CROSSROAD

The path of life is narrow

And the blinded cannot see,

That though it is less traveled

It's the only Way that will set you free.

From the broad, wide way of destruction

That many choose to take,

Worldly desires and fleshly yearnings

Their thirst they try to slake.

Life is fraught with indecision

A spiritual Crossroads we all face,

As we walk along life's journey

Each searching for a place.

Running from a past

That can flow into the present,

What will we make of our future

During the time that we've been lent?

Break free from the chains that bind

Or become slave to images we portray,

Look into the brightness

Or wear a mask for the rest of our days.

What decisions will be made

As we vacillate left to right,

To remain blinded in darkness

Or dance in God's clear light.

Nichole Smith

THE DAY THE WIND CAME TO SCHOOL

There was no joy in room 103
Mrs. Anderson's class today,
The wind had swiftly left its home
And in their classroom played.
It grabbed Earlinda's homework
Whipping it into the air,
Along with Chris's pencil
Now you know *that* wasn't fair!
Nathan lost his jersey
And Ashleigh her hairbrush,
Craig's crayons weren't even safe
As through the room it rushed.
T.K. wrestled with the wind
Using moves from 'Matrix 2',
And Jeremy just limped around
That crafty wind had his shoe!
Meagan remained silent
A minute?...two?...or three?
The wind snatched Timmy's glasses
He couldn't even see.
An eraser left the chalkboard
Narrowly missing Sean,
It landed in Mrs. Clavishaw's mouth
When she opened it to yawn.
All the chaos going on
Had Miss Smith spinning like a top,
Until Mrs. Webster held up her hand
And commanded the wind to "**STOP!**"

THE ISSUES OF MY HEART

The issues of my heart, my LORD, the issues of my heart. You said you'd never leave nor forsake me on this journey and at times, I confess, I have doubted your Word because of the fervency of my trials, the coldness of people, their inherent cruelty…a cruelty that I also possess, but do not want to let have supremacy because You fought all battles at Calvary. Your blood is a timeless blood, it defies all obstacles and barriers. It is an all-powerful substance interlaced with victory. I will not walk around defeated. The notion is a lie of the enemy. Despite and in spite all appearances, I am a daughter of the King! For you are my King, my Adonai, my Savior, my Redeemer, my Shield and Defense. So, when the enemy through people will try to provoke the "Self" to stand tall and defend its nonexistent rights, I will be silent publicly. I will pour out my wounds, my hurts, and disappointments as well as my anger at being misused and abused into my prayer closet…privately. For, how have I been guilty of wounding, hurting, disappointing, using & abusing You? I will be like Hanna and take my petition to You until I hear from on High. I will stand firm upon You, my Rock, O God. I will trust that You know what is best for me even in the midst of overwhelming pain.

THE LOVE I'VE FOUND IN YOU

I've waited all my life
For the love I've found in you,
You took me by surprise
I've found my lifelong friend, it's true.
I love the way you love me
No one else can match your worth,
We were purposed to be together
From the moment of our birth.
Knowing you makes me better
I'll push myself to the limit,
For I cannot imagine
My world without you in it.
Heaven kissed the Earth
And God formed you just for me,
Together, love
Unstoppable is what we'll be.
I look forward to the journey ahead
With you by my side,
Our union is blessed
Because God is our guide.

THE VALUE OF A FRIENDSHIP

Who can measure the depth of love between friends?
Who knows its worth or hidden treasures? Only God.
How can I tell you what you mean to me?
When words just don't seem enough?
Someone who's there through thick and thin
Whenever the going gets tough.
Once in a while God gives a rare gift
That outshines all of the rest,
Our friendship is a witness
That He gives the very best.
The laughter and love, hard times and tears,
Each memory worth it all,
You're there saying, "Come on Nik"
Whenever I trip and fall.
We've climbed mountains, crossed deserts, and endured flames,
In this journey that friendship holds,
I'm always amazed at the strength God gives
As the path before us unfolds.
You always say I "snuck under the radar"
And I laughingly disagree,
The bond forged between us from the Rock
God planned from eternity.
Thank you for times spent
Giving pieces of you,
Sharing your past, baring your soul,
Testifying like you do.
I wish you could step outside of yourself
And experience what I see,
The earnest desire to reflect Christ
And all that He would have you to be.

Nichole Smith

REACHING A MILESTONE

Today is set aside to celebrate
The accomplishment of not one but two,
Friends and family have gathered
To show how much we love you.
Kudos on reaching a milestone
That some never get to see,
With the Almighty as your guide
There's no limit to what you can be.
While pursuing individual goals
He saw fit to bring you together,
As you begin the next phase of your lives
With a love that will not sever.
The sky is the limit
To where your faith can take both of you,
Face each day knowing
Your strength He will renew.
So, congratulations grads
This celebration is worth the wait,
One thing we know for sure
God's blessings are never late!

TINKY

Happy Birthday, Tinky

You have a joy that radiates from within,

Anyone would be blessed

To count you amongst their friends.

God's blessings be upon you

As you celebrate your birth,

Having a loving spirit

Is a treasure of untold worth.

Have a great day

With family and friends,

Wishing you many more

May your blessings never end.

YOU, MY FRIEND

Your friendship is special to me

Words just cannot express

Having someone like you in my life

I know I've really been blessed

You're there for me through ups and downs

Throughout the thick and thin

Making me throw back my head and laugh

Or think of you and grin

The moments we've shared are timeless

Forever etched within my heart

And in the years and eternity ahead

I pray we'll never part.

ABOUT THE AUTHOR

Nichole Smith is a native of Rocky Mount, NC. Her passions are in music, writing plays, poetry and working with children with developmental delays. Nichole is an active member of Christ Gospel Church and a Pen of a Ready Society member. She loves every aspect of writing. Smith's mother instilled a love for reading in her as a child. An ardent love for writing manifested in 11th grade. Writing is her opportunity to let others visualize God's conception. She seeks to glorify God and point others towards Christ through her work. Four of her plays have been performed in Christ Gospel Church of Elkton, Md.

www.ingramcontent.com/pod-product-compliance
Lightning Source LLC
Chambersburg PA
CBHW020946090426
42736CB00010B/1286